Welcome to the *THIS IS AWESOME CUTLERY* FAMILY DEVOTIONALS!

HOW DO WE USE IT?

There are 24 devotionals; 2 for each song on *This is Awesome Cutlery*. You don't need to have listened to the album to use it, but if you have you might get more out of it. We're praying that God will use these sessions to get you more excited about him!

How you use these devotionals is completely up to you. Our main suggestion is to enjoy it, whether that's doing impressions of Captain Awesomeness and Cutlery Boy, dancing along to the songs beforehand, or counting all the adjectives (if you prefer that kind of activity)...!

All the main questions can be answered from the verse(s) printed out. If you're not sure of an answer, why not ask a Christian friend, or someone at your church who teaches the Bible? You could even email us at music@awesomecutlery.com – we don't have all the answers either, but are always happy to help!

WHERE CAN I GET MORE OF THIS STUFF?

Visit awesomecutlery.com and sign up to our mailing list! That way you'll hear about new resources as they come out. You can also go to the 'Resources' tab to see what's currently available.

Please let us know what you think through music@awesomecutlery.com, or on our Facebook page – www.facebook.com/awesomecutlery. We'd love to hear your thoughts!

Love,

GARETH LOH AND DAN ADAMS

(AKA Captain Awesomeness and Cutlery Boy)

GOD IS BIGGER

Family Devotional #1

PRAYER

Father, please help us to be more amazed at how great you are! Amen.

BIBLE VERSE

Read Isaiah 40:12.

"Who has measured the waters in the hollow of his hand, or with the breadth of his hand marked off the heavens?

Who has held the dust of the earth in a basket, or weighed the mountains on the scales and the hills in a balance?"

I just tried to put a mountain in my scales, but I hurt my arm - those scales are heavy!

GAME

Take it in turns to name something. Each thing needs to be bigger than the one before. Start with "ant".

QUESTIONS

What's the biggest thing you got to?

What are the answers to Isaiah's questions in verse 12?

Why is it good news that God is bigger than anything else? *(Could he help us if there was something bigger than him?)*

Because God is bigger, I'm going to trust him!

PRAYER

Dear Father, we praise you that you are bigger and stronger and more powerful than anything else. Amen.

BRAIN-TEASER

Why is it not enough for God just to be the biggest?
(For an answer, see Family Devotional 2...)

GOD IS BIGGER

Family Devotional #2

PRAYER

Father, please encourage us with your love. Amen

BIBLE VERSES Read Romans 8:38–39.

"For I am convinced that neither death nor life, neither angels nor demons, neither the present nor the future, nor any powers, neither height nor depth, nor anything else in all creation, will be able to separate us from the love of God that is in Christ Jesus our Lord."

CHALLENGE

Look at the list for 15 seconds (or read it aloud twice). Can you remember it all between you?

Well, that's a very long list. I got a bit tired just reading it!

QUESTIONS

Where does Paul (the writer of Romans) remind us that God's love is found? *(In which person?)*

Why does he list all these things?

Why is it good news for us that God is big and loving? *(What if he was big but not loving? What if he was loving but not big?)*

Oh, that's why the song says "God is bigger" and "God is loving". It all makes sense now. Does that make me a genius?

PRAYER

Dear Father, thank you so much that nothing can separate us from your powerful love! Amen.

IT'S A NEW NEW DAY

Family Devotional #3

PRAYER

Why not use some words from *It's a New New Day*? It's one big prayer!

BIBLE VERSES

Read Lamentations 3:22–23.

"Because of the Lord's great love we are not consumed, for his compassions never fail. They are new every morning; great is your faithfulness."

BRAIN-TEASER

What's the most important part of your mornings? Why?

QUESTIONS

In the verses, what does God give us each morning?

Hmm. Maybe loading up my Cutlery Belt. If I don't have that, I'm just "Boy"!

Why is that a great thing for us to remember? *(What if we didn't know that God will be kind tomorrow?)*

I needed a dictionary to help me understand a word here. Then I needed Cutlery Boy to help me understand the dictionary. Teamwork.

PRAYER

Dear Father, thank you that you are kind to us every day. Help us to rely on you more than clothes, our house, or breakfast! Amen.

IT'S A NEW NEW DAY

Family Devotional #4

PRAYER

Father God, thank you for your love and compassion! Please help us to know you more. Amen.

HMMM...

If you could only do one thing today, what would it be? Why?

That's a tough one! Can I get back to you with an answer tomorrow?

BIBLE VERSES

Read Matthew 6:31–33.

"So do not worry, saying, 'What shall we eat?' or 'What shall we drink?' or 'What shall we wear?' For the pagans run after all these things, and your heavenly Father knows that you need them. But seek first his kingdom and his righteousness, and all these things will be given to you as well."

QUESTIONS

What things does Jesus tell us not to do today?

Hmm. Sometimes I worry too much. That makes me worried. Oh no! Now I'm even more worried!

QUESTIONS

So what does Jesus tell us to do instead? Why do we not need to worry? *(For more on this, look up verse 26 in the same chapter.)*

Think about something that worries you. How can you seek God in that situation?

PRAYER

Heavenly Father, thank you that you know what we need. Help us to trust you and live for you. Amen.

GOD MADE EVERYTHING

Family Devotional #5

PRAYER

Heavenly Father, thank you for making everything. Help us to enjoy you more! Amen.

CHALLENGE

Which bit of *God made everything* do you know best? Prove it!

Easy - there's a prawn prawn prawn lawn prawn. I think I repeated myself once, but that's okay.

BIBLE VERSES

Read John 1:1–3.

"In the beginning was the Word, and the Word was with God, and the Word was God. He was with God in the beginning. Through him all things were made; without him nothing was made that has been made."

QUESTIONS

Who, or what, do you think the Word is? Why?
(Clue: look at John 1:17–18)

What different things do these verses tell us about him?

Which of these things makes you go "WOW!" the most?

BRAIN-TEASER

If you make a sandwich, doesn't that mean God didn't make it?

If you do make a sandwich, make sure you use a knife to spread the filling carefully and evenly!

PRAYER

Dear Father, thank you for making us and giving us everything we have. Amen.

GOD MADE EVERYTHING

Family Devotional #6

PRAYER

Heavenly Father, thank you for another day to love you and love others! Amen.

HMMM...

What's the best thing you've ever made?

I've made Cutlery Boy a birthday present - it's a cape made entirely out of ham. Deliciously practical.

BIBLE VERSE

Read Revelation 4:11.

"You are worthy our Lord and God to receive glory and honour and power, for you created all things, and by your will they were created and have their being."

I wonder if I can give glory to God for my heroic acts, such as... arranging forks in size order?

QUESTION

What does the verse say God should get? How would you put that in your own words?

Why does God deserve that?

How can we give glory to God in what we say and do?

PRAYER

Dear Father, you are worthy to receive glory and honour and power. Help us to praise you! Amen

GOD'S PEOPLE IN GOD'S PLACE

Family Devotional #7

PRAYER

Heavenly Father, thank you for being kind to us. Help us to know you better. Amen.

HMMM...

What's the furthest you've travelled? Why did you go there?

Imagine if God told me to leave home... who would make my packed lunch each day?

BIBLE VERSES

Read Genesis 12:1–2, 7.

"The Lord had said to Abram, 'Go from your country, your people and your father's household to the land I will show you. I will make you into a great nation, and I will bless you; I will make your name great, and you will be a blessing.' ... The Lord appeared to Abram and said, 'To your offspring I will give this land.'"

QUESTIONS

What did God tell Abram to do?

Why would that have been hard to obey?

What does God promise Abram?

It's a big promise – do you think God could keep it?

BONUS: Can you think of any Bible stories that show how God kept his promise to Abram?

PRAYER

Father, thank you for your loving promises. Thank you that you bless us. Amen.

GOD'S PEOPLE IN GOD'S PLACE

Family Devotional #8

PRAYER

Dear Father, thank you for making promises. Help us to trust you. Amen.

HMMM...

What do you think heaven will be like?

BIBLE VERSES Read Revelation 21:2–4.

"I saw the Holy City, the new Jerusalem, coming down out of heaven from God, prepared as a bride beautifully dressed for her husband. And I heard a loud voice from the throne saying, 'Look! God's dwelling place is now among the people, and he will dwell with them. They will be his people, and God himself will be with them and be their God. He will wipe every tear from their eyes. There will be no more death or mourning or crying or pain, for the old order of things has passed away.'"

A city as a bride? That would need to be a big dress.

QUESTIONS

What do these verses tell us about God's people, God's place, God's rule, and God's blessing?

What will it be like living with God in heaven?

How does this make you feel?

I was really excited when I found out that a spork is actually a thing, but this is on another level!

PRAYER

Father, thank you so much for what you are going to do one day. Help us to look forward to heaven! Amen.

ALL AROUND THE WORLD

Family Devotional #9

PRAYER

Heavenly Father, thank you for another day to live for you. Amen.

HMMM...

Who is the most powerful person in the world right now?

BIBLE VERSE

Read Philippians 2:9-11a.

"Therefore God exalted him to the highest place and gave him the name that is above every name, that at the name of Jesus every knee should bow, in heaven and on earth and under the earth, and every tongue acknowledge that Jesus Christ is Lord."

QUESTIONS

Where is Jesus now?

What does it mean that Jesus' name is "above every name"?

What does this mean about Jesus and us?

It means I'm not in charge anymore... that might be a good thing, I sometimes make tiny, terrible mistakes.

QUESTION

How can you show that Jesus is Lord by the way you live today?

PRAYER

Heavenly Father, you have made Jesus our Lord. Help us to serve him. Amen.

ALL AROUND THE WORLD

Family Devotional #10

PRAYER

Father God, thank you for showing us that Jesus is Lord.

HMMM...

What's more important - saying or doing?

What about saying you're doing something? Is that the best of all?

BIBLE VERSE

Read Matthew 7:21.

"Not everyone who says to me, 'Lord, Lord,' will enter the kingdom of heaven, but only the one who does the will of my Father who is in heaven."

QUESTIONS

What does Jesus think is more important – saying or doing?

Why is it not enough just to say 'Jesus is Lord'?

Oh, that means just singing songs about God isn't enough. If we believe Jesus is Lord, we'll live differently too!

QUESTION

Where in your life does your saying not match your doing? Ask God to help you live it out!

PRAYER

Heavenly Father, help us to show Jesus is Lord in the way we live. Amen.

IT'S A LIGHT AND A HAMMER

Family Devotional #11

PRAYER

Father, we praise you for this day. Help us to know you more in it. Amen.

BIBLE VERSE

Read Psalm 119:105.

"Your word is a lamp for my feet, a light on my path."

CHALLENGE

If you left your house with your eyes closed, how far could you make it safely?

Maybe I could make it to the end of the garden. It depends on whether Captain had tidied up all his stuff.

QUESTIONS

How does Psalm 119:105 say God's word helps us?

So if someone tries to live without listening to God, what is going to happen to them?

QUESTION

Can you think of a way God's word helps us know how to live?

One time I walked around in the dark, and I kept falling over. Then I realised my mask had slipped over my eyes.

PRAYER

Heavenly Father, thank you that you show us how to live. Please help us to follow the light of your word. Amen.

IT'S A LIGHT AND A HAMMER

Family Devotional #12

PRAYER

Heavenly Father, thank you for speaking to us. Help us to know what you're saying. Amen.

HMMM...

Name a book that's helped you to be better at something. What can you do after reading it?

I read "How to Speak English". It me helped many lots.

BIBLE VERSE

Read 2 Timothy 3:16.

"All Scripture is God-breathed and is useful for teaching, rebuking, correcting and training in righteousness."

QUESTIONS

What's so special about where the Bible comes from?

Why does that mean we can trust the Bible?

What can the Bible help us to do?

This sounds even more useful than my manual "How to organise your grapefruit spoons!" And that's a pretty useful manual.

PRAYER

Father, please help us to listen to your word, and to be changed by it. Amen.

FATHER, YOU ARE KING OF HEAVEN

Family Devotional #13

PRAYER

You can use the words of *Father you are King of Heaven* as a prayer.

HMMM...

Think of some things you need each day – who is the best person to ask for each one?

I tend to ask my parents. They always seem to know what's best, like where I should store my spatulas.

BIBLE VERSES Read Matthew 6:9–13.

"This, then, is how you should pray:
'Our Father in heaven, hallowed be your name, your kingdom come, your will be done, on earth as it is in heaven. Give us today our daily bread. And forgive us our debts, as we also have forgiven our debtors. And lead us not into temptation, but deliver us from the evil one.'"

QUESTION

Jesus says we can call God "Father". How does that encourage us to pray?

Praying to a God who is also your heavenly Dad is one of the most amazing things I've ever heard.

QUESTIONS

Are the first requests in the prayer about us or about God?

Why do you think that is?

In what ways can we pray for God's name to be honoured and for his kingdom to grow?

PRAYER

Heavenly Father, thank you that you hear our prayers. We pray people all over the world will trust you. Amen.

FATHER, YOU ARE KING OF HEAVEN

Family Devotional #14

PRAYER

Use Matthew 6:9–13 as your prayer!

"This, then, is how you should pray:

'Our Father in heaven, hallowed be your name, your kingdom come, your will be done, on earth as it is in heaven. Give us today our daily bread. And forgive us our debts, as we also have forgiven our debtors. And lead us not into temptation, but deliver us from the evil one.'"

If you're gluten-free, do you have to ask God for different food?

It's hard to forgive other people. Especially when they're the bad guys.

HMMM...

How much can we live without God's help? Why do you think that?

QUESTIONS

In your own words, what should we ask God to help us with?

What does that mean for how much we depend on God?

Why do you think God asks us to pray for these things?

PRAYER

Heavenly Father, please give us what we need today. Amen.

GOD SHOWED US HIS LOVE

Family Devotional #15

PRAYER

Heavenly Father, thank you for your kindness to us. Amen.

CHALLENGE

Think of something really loving you could do for someone next to you *(and do it later!)*

I like to go for High Fives. Or, if I really love someone, High Tens. That's mathematically double the love.

BIBLE VERSE Read Romans 5:8.

"But God demonstrates his own love for us in this: while we were still sinners, Christ died for us."

A sinner? Yes, I suppose I am. We all do things that are wrong.

QUESTIONS

How did God show his love for us?

What were we like when God did that for us?

Why does that mean his love must be HUGE?

QUESTIONS

How do you know God loves you?

How much does he love you?

PRAYER

Father God, we're sorry for our sin. We praise you for loving us so much! Amen.

GOD SHOWED US HIS LOVE

Family Devotional #16

PRAYER

Dear Father, thank you that you sent Jesus for us. Help us to rejoice in your love! Amen.

BIBLE VERSE Read Romans 5:10.

"For if, while we were God's enemies, we were reconciled to him through the death of his Son, how much more, having been reconciled, shall we be saved through his life!"

HMMM...

How do people treat their enemies?

I wouldn't give treats to any of my enemies. They're MY treats.

QUESTIONS

What does this verse say we were?

What did God do for us?

(If enemies become friends, they are "reconciled".)

What is God going to do for us in the future?

How do we know we will be saved?

That's even more secure than my Cutlery Belt. And that stays up even when my trousers fall down. I mean, if they ever did fall down.

PRAYER

Heavenly Father, thank you that your friends can be sure they are completely saved. Amen.

JUSTIFIED

Family Devotional #17

PRAYER

Father God, thank you for your love for us each day. Amen.

BIBLE VERSES

Read Romans 3:23–24

"For all have sinned and fall short of the glory of God, and all are justified freely by his grace through the redemption that came by Christ Jesus."

CHALLENGE

(Maybe talk about it now, try it later!)

Take turns throwing something to the moon. Who gets closest? Does it matter?

I threw an egg up, but I forgot about it straight away. It landed on my head and now the yolk's on me. And the white is. All of it, really.

QUESTIONS

Which of us have managed to reach God's glory ourselves?

How then can we be free?

Remember - "justified" means "made right with God", just as if we'd lived Jesus' life!

QUESTION

How can someone be justified?

Clue: is it a gift or do we earn it?

PRAYER

Dear Father, thank you for freely justifying us through Jesus! Amen.

JUSTIFIED

Family Devotional #18

PRAYER

Heavenly Father, we praise you for the gifts you have given us. Amen.

MEMORY CHALLENGE

From what we've looked at so far, what has God done for us?

> Ah, a memory cha... Hmm. I've forgotten the last word. Channel? Chapel? Champagne? Cha-cha? It's one of those.

BIBLE VERSE

Read Romans 5:1.

"Therefore, since we have been justified through faith, we have peace with God through our Lord Jesus Christ."

QUESTIONS

How can we be justified?

If someone is justified, what do they have with God?

If you trust in Jesus, how does God feel about you right now?

> That's such a long way from being God's enemies! Amazing!

PRAYER

Father God, help us to trust in Jesus as the one who brings us peace with you. Amen.

ENTER THROUGH THE NARROW GATE

Family Devotional #19

PRAYER

Father God, help us to listen carefully to your words. Amen.

HMMM...

What big decisions will you make in your life?

I made a big decision this morning - teaspoon, or tablespoon? I went with a tablespoon... of sugar.

BIBLE VERSES Read Matthew 7:13–14

"Enter through the narrow gate. For wide is the gate and broad is the road that leads to destruction, and many enter through it. But small is the gate and narrow the road that leads to life, and only a few find it."

QUESTIONS

What are the two options Jesus gives in the verses?

Why do many people go on the broad road?

Maybe they don't know where's it's going - we should warn them!

QUESTION

Where do the two options end? Which is best?

PRAYER

Dear Father, please help us to walk the narrow road, even when it's hard. Amen.

ENTER THROUGH THE NARROW GATE

Family Devotional #20

PRAYER

Heavenly Father, help us to love you like you love us. Amen.

BIBLE VERSE Read Matthew 7:24

"Therefore everyone who hears these words of mine and puts them into practice is like a wise man who built his house on the rock."

CHALLENGE

What's the worst thing you can think of to build a house on?

Jelly. No wait, at least you could eat it. But of course, I would never do that.

QUESTION

What does it look like to build your life on Jesus' words?

What two things must a wise person do with Jesus' words?

I thought it was just going to be "listen to Jesus", but it's more than that!

QUESTION

How can you do those two things today?

PRAYER

Father God, thank you that you speak to us. Help us to hear and obey. Amen.

A LONG LONG LONG LONG TIME AGO

Family Devotional #21

PRAYER

Heavenly Father, help us to know your faithfulness as we look at your word. Amen

HMMM...

If you were going to rule a country, what sort of king or queen would you be?

I would make all my advisers work to invent something to eat soup with noodles in. It's impossible!

BIBLE VERSES

Read 2 Samuel 7:11b–13 (where God is speaking to King Davi

"The LORD declares to you that the LORD himself will establish a house for you: when your days are over and you rest with your ancestors, I will raise up your offspring to succeed you, your own flesh and blood, and I will establish his kingdom. He is the one who will build a house for my Name, and I will establish the throne of his kingdom for ever."

QUESTIONS

What does God say he is going to give King David?

How long will this new king rule for?

I was going to say "for ever", but that seems like quite a long time. Now I'm confused and need a hug.

QUESTION

Who do you think God was talking about?

PRAYER

Father, thank you that you promised to send your Son Jesus to be king forever! Amen

A LONG LONG LONG LONG TIME AGO

Family Devotional #22

PRAYER

Dear Father, help us to enjoy your word today. Amen.

CHALLENGE

Name some important babies.

Well, me when I was a baby. Jelly Babies. And now I've run out of ideas.

BIBLE VERSES

Read Luke 1:30–32

"But the angel said to her, 'Do not be afraid, Mary, you have found favour with God. You will conceive and give birth to a son, and you are to call him Jesus. He will be great and will be called the Son of the Most High. The Lord God will give him the throne of his father David.'"

QUESTIONS

What does the angel say about Jesus?

How does that link back to God's promise to David in 2 Samuel 7:11b–13?

I think it's really clever how the Bible story fits together.

QUESTION

How important is Jesus and why?

PRAYER

Father God, we praise you for Jesus and all you've done through him! Amen.

HE HAS RISEN!

Family Devotional #23

PRAYER

Heavenly Father, thank you for a new day – help us to worship you. Amen.

HMM...

How does it feel to get into trouble for something that wasn't your fault?

Terrible, it feels so unfair! Once, someone sat on a fork, and I got all the blame, just because I left a fork on a chair. Oh, wait.

BIBLE VERSES

Read Luke 23:33–34a

"When they came to the place called the Skull, they crucified him there, along with the criminals – one on his right, the other on his left. Jesus said, 'Father, forgive them, for they do not know what they are doing.'"

I almost can't believe they did that to Jesus... except the Bible says they did.

QUESTIONS

What does Jesus want for the people crucifying him (and what does he want for us too)?

What do these verses make you want to say to God?

BRAIN-TEASER

Jesus didn't deserve to be crucified. So why did God let that happen?

PRAYER

Use the things you've just said to pray to God.

HE HAS RISEN!

Family Devotional #24

PRAYER

Father God, help us to know you and love you more! Amen.

BIBLE VERSES

Read Luke 24:36b–41

"Jesus himself stood among them and said to them, 'Peace be with you.' They were startled and frightened, thinking they saw a ghost. He said to them, 'Why are you troubled, and why do doubts rise in your minds? Look at my hands and my feet. It is I myself! Touch me and see; a ghost does not have flesh and bones, as you see I have.' When he had said this, he showed them his hands and feet. And while they still did not believe it because of joy and amazement, he asked them, 'Do you have anything here to eat?'"

I like that bit about asking for food! I would have been so happy I wouldn't have even minded if he ate without a fork!

QUESTION

Imagine being there! How would you feel when Jesus said these things?

I would feel really really really super really mega super happy. Except even more than that.

QUESTIONS

How many things in the story show us Jesus really was alive again?

How can we be sure that death is defeated? What does that mean for us?

PRAYER

Heavenly Father, we praise you for the wonderful news that Jesus is alive! Help us to worship him. Amen.

RECOMMENDED RESOURCES AVAILABLE FROM 10OFTHOSE.COM

Here are a few more resources from other people that we've enjoyed. Why not pick one to try next?

Long Story Short / Old Story New

Marty Machowski
Ten-minute devotions to draw your family to God.

Beginning with God / Bake Through The Bible

Various authors, Good Book Company
Especially good for preschoolers!

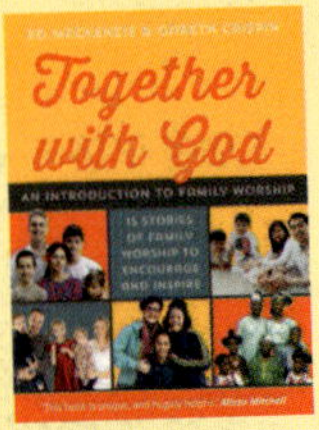

Together with God

Gareth Crispin and Ed Mackenzie
An introduction to family worship featuring 15 stories of how families worship and pray together at home.

XTB / Table Talk

Good Book Company
Bible reading notes for 7-11s, plus questions to talk about as a family.

What have you found helpful? Let us know so we can help spread the word!

music@awesomecutlery.com facebook.com/awesomecutlery

CAPTAIN
AWESOMEness